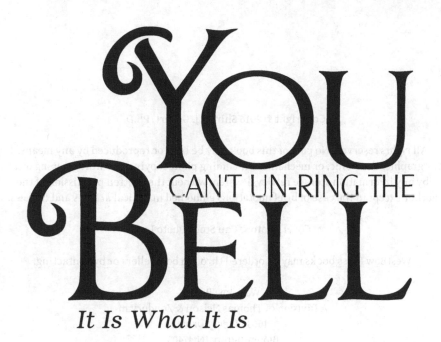

YOU
CAN'T UN-RING THE
BELL

It Is What It Is

Shirley J. Gilbert, Ph.D.

WestBow
PRESS®
A DIVISION OF THOMAS NELSON
& ZONDERVAN

WestBow Press books may be ordered through booksellers or by contacting:

WestBow Press
A Division of Thomas Nelson & Zondervan
1663 Liberty Drive
Bloomington, IN 47403
www.westbowpress.com
1 (866) 928-1240

ISBN: 978-1-5127-3431-7 (sc)
ISBN: 978-1-5127-3432-4 (e)

Print information available on the last page.

WestBow Press rev. date: 03/14/2016

DEDICATION

Bells, in this book, are a metaphor for the challenges we experience in our lives. As I dedicate this book to my little grandson, James, it is my prayer that he will grow up taking the bells seriously, that they enrich his life and encourage him to make endless healthy choices.

CONTENTS

INTRODUCTION

I have spent a lifetime trying to be helpful to others, trying to listen without judgment, making interventions and guiding a process that leads to empowerment and strength. The learning curve has been steep. I could have chosen an easier profession, and some days wish I had! These pages hold information for which people paid $200 an hour. They have been summarized in this book and are reviewed in the final chapter.

All of the first words of each chapter title begin with an action word. That is the key to this book: taking action. Short of acting on what we know, what is the point in knowing? That is the tricky part.

Information is power, but knowing isn't doing. People should write about what they know. This is what I know, after decades of treating people with serious trauma.

Since I have retired, I've had a lot of time to think about and process the bells in my own life. I decided to write this book to share concepts I believe can make a meaningful difference in life, if we take them seriously. It has taken me outside my comfort zone to write it. Reflecting on painful bells is serious business. Nonetheless, I invite you to do exactly that so that you can manage them and move on without carrying unnecessary baggage.

This is a book about reality, about getting real about your life. It has challenged me to be real, open and honest about my own. In fact, I have come to realize it doesn't matter how many degrees you have, how much money you have, how much knowledge you have. It's all about the choices we make, no matter what! The whole point is applying what we know, using it to make a positive difference in someone's life, hopefully our own. I am a firm believer in making changes due to knowledge and wisdom.

I have seen it. I have lived it. Often, when people know better, they do better. However, knowing isn't always doing!

Education and experience can be powerful teachers. We simply can't apply what we don't know. It's hard enough to apply what we do know.

A large part of my motivation to write this book has to do with the state of the world, as I see it, filled with depression, anger, hopelessness, mental illness, addictions, hatred, people giving up, domestic violence, suicide, mass shootings, animal and child abuse. We have got to turn this around, and we can.

I believe more people need to be thinking, talking about and creating change. We need to take serious pause at the condition of our world. People are giving up. We seem way overdue in addressing solutions and making positive changes. It all has to start with each one of us.

I am a mental health expert. I hold four college degrees (including two Ph.D.'s 20 years apart) and have had several licenses to practice psychology in more than one State. I have been an invited guest speaker at the FBI Headquarters in Quantico and was part of the Columbine massacre mental health team. I have worked with insane children and violent offenders. I have spent years in private practice and have seen the human condition at its worst.

In addition to my lengthy years of education and training, my greatest strength has been my simple faith in a loving God who is the Source of my power to face the daily life challenges of the bells. He has promised that He has a plan for our lives "a plan for good and not for evil, to give us a future and a hope." We either believe that or we don't. I believe it.

My faith is what has motivated and enabled me to do my work in the field of mental health and write this book. I pray you will find it meaningful and helpful in managing your life as I lay out specific tools that can help you make changes in how you manage the bells in your life.

S.J. Gilbert, Ph.D.

Carmel, CA

January, 2016

"Whole faith in a sovereign God enables us to step when we cannot see, trust what we cannot trace, and undergo what we may not understand."

(Haddon Robinson)

CHAPTER ONE
Ringing of the Bells

> "Our lives are shaped by those who love us and those who have refused to love us."(John Powell, WHY AM I AFRAID TO TELL YOU WHO I AM?)

As I stated, bells, in this book, are a metaphor for the challenges we experience in our lives. They represent the events, chosen and unchosen, each of us faces.

The bells have the power to chew us up and spit us out. Sometimes they ring very quietly and we may not even hear them, or sometimes we ignore them, often to our detriment.

As soon as we leave the womb, the bells begin to ring. We learn that they can symbolize something very positive or they can be a formidable opponent. I have chosen to write about the challenges of the bells, the events in our lives which often create pain or some kind of challenge for us.

Because of the bells, many of us walk with a limp. That is, no one escapes the bells. Things happen to all of us that we can't undo. Sometimes we ring the bell and create problems for ourselves, sometimes others ring the bell. No matter who rings the bell, it often creates challenges and pain and we end up having to deal with what we can't change. Often, it is out of our control, chosen or unchosen. It is what it is.

Examples of the bell ringing could include the ring of loss, the ring of failure, the ring of cancer, the ring of parent-child conflicts, the ring of divorce, the ring of addiction and death and so many other life issues. The traumas of losing a child, ending a marriage, losing a job, poverty, homelessness, death of a loved one, bankruptcy, mental or terminal illness, being the victim of a hate crime, rape, violence, the list goes on and on. Life is difficult!

Every day, people struggle to find answers to their pain and carry trauma which sometimes feels impossible and even overwhelming. Sometimes it feels as though we are looking up to see the bottom! Their mantra becomes, "What's the use?" Sometimes people simply give up. Sometimes our defenses are not strong enough to protect us. Sometimes we don't want to be protected. We just want revenge!

Being in the helping role can create many challenges. I once came upon an anonymous posting, to this effect.

It read:

I hold the hands of people I never touch. I provide comfort to people I never embrace. I watch people walk into bricks walls, the same ones over and over again, and I coax them to turn around and try to walk in a different direction, People rarely see me gladly. As a rule, I catch the residue of their despair. I see people who are broken, and people who only think they are broken. I see people who have had their faces rubbed in their failures. I see weak people wanting anesthesia and strong people who wonder what they have done to make such an enemy of fate. I am often the final pit stop people take before they crawl across the finish line that is marked, "I give up." Some people beg me to help. Some dare me to help. Sometimes they look the same. Some days I'm invigorated by it all, some days I'm numbed and sometimes I just end up hating everyone....(Anonymous)

Some people appear to have had very easy lives. They grew up in a stable, loving family with well-adjusted parents and siblings. They had plenty of money, friends, lived in a good neighborhood, had a good support system. Their reality is very different than another who experienced none of this. So, the challenge of confronting troublesome bells is experienced very differently by these different people. To some, it feels like fantasy land that we can be empowered to confront the bells. Often, we feel powerless, angry, have run out of places to put our frustration and conclude that life is simply unfair. Some people use this line of thinking to adopt a lifestyle of hatred, bitterness and destruction. Their lifestyle is revenge. This is anti-social thinking and the root of many heinous crimes.

All of us have had life experiences which have created painful markers in our journey that have impacted and changed us. Frequently, we look for a quick fix, something that will make us feel better, some kind of immediate gratification that numbs our pain. This is a very normal and common response. No one likes being in pain. Addictions to drugs, sex, power, money, work, food are not the answer, but their immediate gratification provide comfort and a sense of relief at the time. Turning to them is understandable; however, often, they become a bigger problem than what they were designed to help us avoid. Addictions of any kind are dangerous and far reaching. They can be very difficult to treat.

Dysfunction and evil come in many attractive forms. Sometimes we just want to get even with the person that caused us pain. But, hurting others solves nothing. I've heard it said that when we exercise our anger, it's like drinking poison and expecting the other person to die. We don't heal by hurting others.

Understanding that life will always be full of challenges is a fact we need to get used to and learn to manage. It is a prerequisite to having some semblance of mental health. Coming to terms with what we wish never was is a mark of emotional health.

We can't change our past, but we can learn to come to terms with it, no matter what, and move on. This process often feels very alone and we may feel misunderstood by those closest to us as we seek to make changes. We are challenged with the difficulty to try to understand and accept our pain as another lesson learned and move on. This is sometimes very hard to do. If we are not able to do it, then we carry it as unfinished business, a burden which can become very heavy and self-debilitating. That decision often comes with a very heavy price tag. It can be lethal to our health and our relationships, including our children.

Feeling judged can be lethal. It is hard not to let the behavior of others destroy our inner peace--a husband who walks out of your life, a child who decides he doesn't like you and doesn't want you in his life anymore, a pastor who reigns down his wrath on you. It's hard to believe that our value does not decrease because someone else doesn't believe in us.

Also, we should never have to beg to be a part of anyone's life. If they don't recognize our value, we may be better off without them. The key is believing in ourselves. This is not always easy to do. Relationships are complex and end for all sorts of reasons. No matter what the reason, we need to take responsibility for our part, learn the lesson, and move on!

As we get stuck on dysfunctional detours, we often spend a lifetime trying to defend our unhealthy actions, mostly to ourselves. In the meantime, we suffer consequences of our choices as does everyone else involved with us. Pain is often contagious.

I watched the agony of my Aunt as she struggled for a lifetime with the death of her only son who died of a heroin overdose at the age of 18. There have been other tragedies in our family which have created enormous and painful scars. This is likely true for many families. The issue is not so much the trauma as it is the response to the trauma. We always have a choice about our response, although it seldom feels that way.

Clearly, life really isn't fair. It is insane to expect it will ever be fair. Sometimes, it feels the pain just keeps coming. Yes, we all have traumatic examples. We can expect them. We need to be prepared to meet those challenges head-on because we can always count on them showing up.

From broken relationships to traumatic memories, the challenge is ours to come to terms. We can either become bitter or better. The choice is ours. I've watched too many people slip into the victim role rather than becoming proactive in meeting difficult challenges. We need to try to learn from them and become a better person and learn the lesson.

It is not uncommon for people to construct a mask. We try to present ourselves to the world as the person we really are but are often tempted to present as the person we wish we were, because we give others far too much power to judge us.

Most of us are not secure enough to be vulnerable or to operate outside of our comfort zone. We need to really understand the reality that we cannot un-ring the bells of our life experiences and who we have become as a result. Not even God can un-ring the bell!!

Some of my own sharp edges have become smoother, but some will never be as resolved as I might wish. Change comes slowly. Changing thoughts, feelings and behaviors are the hardest work I know. Healing is a process, not an event. There will always be unfinished business. In fact, I have worked on some of my own issues for decades

I once had an experience on a beach I rarely frequent where I encountered a striking-looking woman standing by herself, looking pensively out to the ocean. Spontaneously, I approached her and we started a conversation. Within minutes, she disclosed she had driven more than 100 miles to reach the beach, hoping for some relief from her painful feelings of rejection from her adopted son. We spoke at length as I could relate to her pain and shared my thoughts with her.

What a joy to bring a new baby home from the hospital, a precious bundle of love.

We watch them grow up and have a million precious memories of loving times with them. Adoptive children are special in so many ways that they often do not understand. For them it sometimes translates that the person who should have been their greatest nurturer gave them away. They see themselves as abandoned, not chosen. The mother of an adopted child who ends up being rejected is filled with feelings of failure and guilt. Sometimes, for reasons we don't understand, we become aware of painful emotional distance with our children we neither understand nor know how to fix. If we are not careful, we can allow those feelings to shred our heart. Parent-child pain seems to be especially excruciating. Sometimes, in spite of our best efforts, we can't seem to find the road to healing that relationship. It reminds me of an old country song that says, "My heart keeps paying you back for things it didn't do." Those were my feelings.

It takes both people to want a relationship to work. We mustn't give up. Sometimes we just have to give it back to God and let Him work His plan. We never know what might turn it around. We have to keep the faith, and move on--easy to say, hard to do!

Simply listening to her story seemed to help her. I was reminded again of how it helps all of us to just have someone who will really listen to us when we need to be heard. We don't need to be rich, beautiful or have all the answers in order to help others, we just need to be there. God gave us one mouth and two ears. The world needs more listeners......not to 'fix' anything, but just to listen and try to 'get it.' It helps people feel not so alone, one of the major triggers of suicide. I think we need to try to be there for others, not because of personal gain, but because we can possibly plant a seed of hope that can make a difference in someone's life.

I have felt the pain of too many who have decided to take their lives, many of them Christians. These deaths have been especially painful.

I'm so grateful for all those who have taken time for me, and for the difference they have made in my life, many of them teachers. Those people have made all the difference in my capacity to even recognize choices I didn't realize were available to me. Everyone is a teacher! Everyone has something to teach us!

Everyone can identify something in their life they wish they could undo. If only it were that easy. We live with the circumstances of our lives and the choices we make to respond. In fact, we ARE our choices. There are likely at least a million people who would take back many decisions if they could. I am among them.

We even have to live with facts of our lives we did not create!!! It feels downright unfair for those who got stuck with poor health, adoption, physical, genetic and emotional disabilities, mentally ill parents, addictions, victims of abuse, poverty, violence, and so many other forms of traumatic experiences.

I have learned that it is O.K. to feel angry about things that happen in our lives. In fact, I think the road to health and forgiveness requires that we first pass through our anger, sometimes rage. I remember one of the worst events in my life where I found myself thinking: "I hate you so much, I can't find enough hate to hate you." I carried those feelings for far too long. Owning those feelings was the beginning of changing them. This was a valuable lesson for me and helped me to move on. First I had to get honest before I could work on problem-solving the challenge and the changes I needed to make.

As a Clinical Psychologist, I have spent a good portion of my life trying to help others come to terms with their pain. I have learned that, in fact, everyone has their own version of reality. This makes the helping process even more complicated. Before I did this, however, I had to work on what seemed like endless challenges in my own life. I needed to come to terms with my own traumas. I knew if I didn't, I could never help anyone else with theirs. Coming to terms with not being able to un-ring the bell is one of the greatest challenges I've ever faced. I've also learned that trying to avoid the pain by going around it will never get me where I want to be—healthier, happier, more sane, at peace. Making friends with the concept of acceptance and peace can work wonders for us, especially if we seek the help of the Prince of Peace.

As I said, sometimes we seek detours that include drugs, alcohol, sex, exercise, education, power, desperate attempts to find a partner who will "fix it," plastic surgery, addictions of one sort or another—anything to help us avoid the pain and numb out. Sometimes we lash out at others, somehow believing this will make us feel better. It only makes it much worse. It becomes one more thing to make us feel guilty.

Many of us choose a life we think will keep us safe. We choose safe people and only share surface information with others. John Powell in his book, <u>Why Am I Afraid to Tell you Who I am?</u> says the reason we don't tell others who we are is because if they don't like us, it's all we've got!!!

People choose all kinds of ways to avoid reality. We ignore family for many reasons. ("If only I could relate to the people I'm related to?"). I have a family member I have not spoken with in years, not for lack of caring. Letting go of toxic relationships is often a very painful and complex process.

But, wherever we go, there we are! We bring it all with us. It IS us. We must remember that light comes from the inside. We can't ask the darkness to leave without turning on the light. We have to not only make the decision for change, we must have a commitment to make the changes. This takes time, energy, courage and determination. We have to choose how to manage our challenges. There exist many options--anger/rage, getting even, addictions, therapy, etc.

While we can't un-ring the bell, we can make it quieter!! We can choose not to hear it so loudly. We can even turn around and face it. We can turn it down as we learn to accept and turn up the positive thoughts, events, goals and people in our lives, as we learn to reframe it. We can stop giving it so much power!

We can change the focus of the message in our minds. We CAN find a way to go on that is productive and create a better life for ourselves and others, if we're willing to do the work to make it happen.

It is all within our power of choosing. We can have a past where we no longer live! It IS possible to do this. We are not doomed to depression and addictions because of our trauma, but it will not happen automatically. We must work at it. We must want it a lot. The bell will always ring it's truth. But, we can reframe our pain if we are serious about committing ourselves to it. The power is ours. There's a big difference between wanting change and being willing to do the work to make it happen!

Think of all the markers in your own life where something happened that changed you. Now think about all the possibilities you have available to you to deal with, change all those negative feelings, and move on. Which of your goals have you let go or given up on? Maybe it's time to re-think that process!

I once spent a week at the Mayo Clinic and was amazed at hearing so many stories of triumph over unbelievable pain and suffering. The human spirit is resilient and amazing.

It is not too late! Our story of "Once upon a time..." the story we repeatedly play over and over in our head about our life begins to crack. Little pieces start to splinter off, and then larger chunks start to fall away and sometimes we get a glimpse of what might have been. At that point, we can choose bitterness at that insight or we can use it to begin to discover an alternative that will lead us to creating a healthy soul and bring about healing and peace. Very few people end up where they thought they would when they started. Our paths weave and change in ways we never dreamed. Yes, as they say, life is what happens to us while we're busy making other plans.

In other words, the choices we make even about unforeseen events hold the keys to how we live our lives. We can reframe the past and make it better, happier, and with hope and happiness, but we can't anticipate every decision we are going to have to make. We can overcome our pain by learning to manage it. We start by taking responsibility for our behavior, and stop blaming others for why we hate our lives. We always have a choice about how we are going to respond. This realization is one of the markers that differentiates mental health from some forms of mental illness.

Each time we decide to reframe the pain associated with the ringing of the bell, we can re-choose our positive response and this reinforces our reality that as we continue to respond positively, our depression lifts, our anger softens, and we start to become new people. I've seen it. I've lived it!'

The world is full of good people. If you can't find one, try to be one! You never know what kind of positive impact you can have on others, and on yourself. Be content with simply planting a seed and pass the baton to someone who may choose to water it. For example, I have made supportive comments on the internet to strangers on social media and have been amazed at their positive responses. Perhaps random acts of kindness really do make a difference.

Will we ever reach that perfect place where everything will be resolved? Of course not. This cannot be the goal. Otherwise, we will simply stay miserable. We may not be great, but we can be the best we are capable of at every stage of our life. Don't wait for someone to bring you flowers. Plant your own garden. Nourish your own soul. Be your own best friend.

When I was age 29, I had three college degrees, three beautiful sons and a husband who was a professional. We were a beautiful family. Many years later, however, I discovered a devastating secret. It was complicated and presented problems for all of us. It was the greatest and most painful reality in my life up to that point. After spending three years in therapy, I realized I had to leave the relationship in order to survive. Every day since, however, I have lived with the fallout of that decision. Nonetheless, it is what it is.

I wish I had understood then what I understand now. I've had to let go of that pain and move on, keep learning, growing and doing my best. We choose, we learn, we manage our choices, and we move on, often with a limp. It is what it is.

CHAPTER TWO
Choosing the Power to Reframe

I am my choices.

You have the power to change your life. Believe it! It can be better, more fulfilling, and more peaceful, but only if you decide to make it happen. There is no one with any magic, no quick fix, no easy or painless way. It takes time. It takes setting goals and staying totally committed to them. It takes discipline in controlling our thoughts. It takes you and I making a decision for making changes and standing by them. Maybe it starts with something as simple as creating simple and random acts of kindness every day, including the way we treat ourselves and the people around us, especially our own family.

The concept of reframing is an exciting tool to learn to use. Reframing refers to concentrating on the same event but choosing to see the reality of it from several different points of view. For example, if one grew up in a very dysfunctional family, one can see that the children in such a family may feel doomed to the same kind of life as their parents. (After all, modelling is the most powerful form of education.) Or, they may learn that they do, in fact, have the power not to make the same choices as their parents and see that they can have a very different kind of life. We see great examples of this all the time. I know that I grew up knowing I wanted a very different kind of life than the one I was living. I held onto hope that one day it would be different. It is!

If only we could find a way to communicate to everyone that God's grace is big enough to cover all the bells and bring about healing and peace. If only we could find a quick fix to empower people to believe in themselves and in their Creator to help them.

This is why people's version of reality is so important. If we don't believe in change, grace, forgiveness or second chances, then our options, as we perceive them, take on a very different and limiting set of choices.

The gift of faith in a loving God is an enormous gift in managing the bells of our lives. He created us and has His hand on our lives. If He wanted us to be someone different or to be born into a different home or to have gifts meant for us, it would have happened. We need to accept what is. That's where we all have to start. It is what it is! Before we can work on making changes, we must look reality hard in the face and accept it, whether we like it or not.

Oftentimes people simply need to be shown where to look to understand the possibility that there is a whole world out there they know nothing about. Instead of resenting the people who seem to have it better than they do, they can begin to start to see that their life does not have to be their negative collection of memories, no matter what their story. They have the power to choose and commit to change. So, if we think we are powerless, then we are!

Speaking of stories, I spent five years working with children who had been removed from their homes by the courts because the problems in their homes were so bad. The children were removed, usually for physical, psychological or sexual reasons. These children had witnessed things and relayed stories that were almost unbearable to hear. In fact, there were times I hoped I could keep from vomiting during a session. It was their reality. It was all they'd ever known. Listening carefully to these little people was a tremendous challenge for me to come to see how they perceived the world and, as a result, see themselves—the challenge to understand their reality. I had to try to really get my brain around the evidence of the forces of evil manifested in these little people. At one point, I remember having to tilt my head back to keep the tears from running down my face as I recalled the Scripture: "....better to have a millstone hung around their neck and be thrown into the deepest sea than to offend one of these little ones..." The children I treated were far beyond "offended." They were broken and I often felt as though I was trying to put

Humpty Dumpty back together again! Clearly, it was the hardest clinical work I ever did.

Part of what made it so hard was that I also had to listen to the stories of mass murderers, pedophiles and rapists. This was extremely difficult for me. As I said earlier, everyone has their own version of reality.

Many of the children were on multiple medications and I sometimes found them in the corner of a dark closet or under a bed, screaming in agony, terrified, and out of control. It was heartbreaking.

In spite of all this, however, I learned that it is easier to fix a broken child than a broken adult.

It was not a pretty picture nor an easy task of helping them move forward. Nonetheless, it was possible and very exciting to watch them take baby steps to begin helping them create a new reality of, "Yes, I can." I watched some of them begin to change and to thrive. These have been some of the most rewarding moments of my life.

When I left a treatment center where I worked for three years, the children made me an album of their pictures with special messages. It is one of my greatest treasures.

Conversely, I have worked in some of the nation's darkest prisons and have listened to the reality of the most mentally ill and the most violent offenders. They have a different reality which often led to the death and destruction of others. The challenge of the bells for them is much harder. They will be paying the consequences of their actions for a lifetime. Nonetheless, many of them were open to understanding there was another way to live.

I taught a class called "Life Skills" and had a waiting list. They were eager to learn. I found so many of them to be bright and motivated. They, however, were late to the party of learning to reframe. Their perceptions of their broken lives made it especially difficult to apply issues of change while in their prison environment. They provided special challenges, but I will never forget the courage and creativeness they demonstrated. If only, someone had shown them a different path earlier in their lives. Many of them had no idea who their biological mother was. Life is not fair. Nonetheless, we live in a world that holds us accountable for our choices, no matter what the circumstances. The bell has rung. It is what it is.

I will not forget seeing purple sticky notes in some of their cells upon which I had written my favorite verse: "God has a plan for you, a plan for good and not for evil, to give you a future and a hope." Some of them were very receptive to hearing and believing such a message.

Part of the process of learning to let go of the destructive forces of the un-ringing of the bell has to do with timing. Children and lifer inmates represent the extremes. The challenges, nonetheless, are equally difficult because change happens slowly, even with insight, for both groups. Nonetheless, reframing is a powerful concept that focuses on the idea of change and change is what most psychologists attempt to help people do. Sometimes it can be as simple as showing someone where to look, but usually it is much more challenging. It requires immense reinforcement. Knowing isn't doing. You can't just have insight into the problem. One must be diligent in applying the solution and reinforce it at every opportunity. This is how change happens! We can't always wait for the perfect time. There is no perfect time. The right time is always "now."

I was part of responding to the crisis at the Columbine High School massacre. Losing a child to murder does not represent a bell that will ever be forgotten. The trauma of evil is a challenge for victims and helpers alike. I remember being at the Littleton Hospital in the room of a teacher from the school who had been brought in by ambulance. As her pulse surged, she was not even registering where she was, let alone the trauma she had just suffered. Or, holding and crying with a young student in the waiting room in excruciating emotional pain because of the death of his best friend. Being in the helping profession sometimes offers extreme challenges which can create vicarious trauma and secondary post-traumatic stress for the caregiver. I experienced it on that horrible day. I knew when it was time for me to stop giving speeches about Columbine. I can still feel that pain.

Pain comes in all forms, at all ages. There is so much pain in the world along with the temptation to simply give up. Many parents model this for their children and so the generations of dysfunctional lives seems unending. The cycle continues: "If we always do what we always did, we'll always get what we always got." Someone has to start making different choices. I am weary of hearing children and adults tell me about the devastating impact of addictions, abuse and suicide on their family.

What a positive difference we could all make if we were committed to helping each other heal. We need to stop competing and have the attitude that we want everyone to feel better. We don't gain self-esteem by comparing ourselves to others and by trying to be better than them. We gain self-esteem by supporting their gifts and reinforcing their strengths. Everyone needs a cheerleader. Sometimes we need to be our own best cheerleader. Depending on others to always give us what we need when we need it usually sets us up for depression and disappointments.

We need to focus on our strengths, not our weaknesses, focus on what is right in our lives, not what's wrong. We need to focus on where we're going, not where we've been. We need to not miss tomorrow looking back at yesterday. We need to stop making judgments and put on our wide-angle lens of possibilities. We need to stop running out of places to put our pain and take up the challenge to deal with it.

I've been encouraged and challenged to have eyes that see the best in people, a heart that forgives the worst, a mind that lets go of the pain and a soul that keeps me centered. These goals are linked to my sanity and well-being. I count on them every day.

CHAPTER THREE
Changing Our Filter

**Most of us are the
carpenters of our own crosses.**

We will never be able to let go of anything unless we learn to change our thoughts, change our filter.

Our behavior is controlled by our thoughts and feelings. We have to find an anchor that balances us, keeps us looking forward and we need to remember that the "what ifs" and "if onlys" will kill us. We must accept what is before we can change. We must stay focused.

Each of us has constructed a filter through which we perceive the world. It is constructed of a totality of our experiences since birth. In essence, our filter is the reality we have constructed, based on our experiences. It controls our perceptions of the world and of ourselves.

It includes our judgments, attitudes, love, compassion, anger, etc. It IS our truth! It IS our perception of reality. It is all based on our interpretations of our experiences. It helps us understand why different people perceive the same event so differently.

For example, I heard someone say, "It's winter, we need to pray for the homeless," to which someone else replied, "It's winter, we must help the homeless find a warm home." These two statements represent very different filters, very different ways of perceiving and doing 'life.' Which one are you?

I am also aware of the difference in the filters of those who take responsibility for their choices compared to those who blame everyone but themselves for the state of their lives. This is the first major construct that needs to change before we can begin to work on our goals.

As long as we are not responsible in the first place, then we have an excuse to blame and never be responsible. We can feel justified in being jaded, negative and hateful. That kind of venom gets spewed in the most evil kind of ways. I have seen the effects. They are horrific. They are deadly, even when the anger is legitimate!

I recently listened to a man describe his experience of his father. He said, "I hate him." I could only imagine the pain he must be carrying to have such feelings.

When we explored this subject at length, I concluded that he wanted and needed things from his father who was not capable of giving his son what he wanted and needed. The son's concept of what love looks like did not match his father's reality of that same concept. My conclusion is that he is wanting something from his father which he does not have to give him. He doesn't "get it." Neither of them get it!

The adult child can either hang on to his bitterness and hatred, or he can change his attitude to understand that he is wanting something from someone who is incapable of giving him what he is demanding. Clearly, the choice is his, and he has made it. He has become the carpenter of his own cross. He feels justified. Sometimes we need to ask ourselves if we'd rather be right or well?

Expectations can be deadly. If we could learn to let go of them, it would diminish a mountain of pain and anger people carry. How do you stay mad at someone who isn't capable of giving you what you need from them? No one heals by hurting others. Some people have no interest in healing, They are only interested in inflicting pain and anguish with their anger, often on animals and children.

People carry burdens of baggage throughout their lives, unnecessarily so!! We often become the carpenters of our own crosses.

A powerful image of this concept comes to mind from the movie, "The Mission." This is the story of a priest who feels so guilty that he constructs an almost impossible mass of heavy irons around his neck which he drags for years to punish himself. One day, he decides to change his reality and releases himself from the heavy massive burden he has carried most of his life. He allows grace to flow into his life and he experiences a kind of freedom he never knew existed. This was the beginning of change in his life, no longer choosing guilt, anger and depression as his best friends. He forgave himself!

That's right, we CHOOSE our emotions! They come from our thoughts, which come from our filter. This is why early education is so critical in teaching our children. We are laying the foundation for how they will live out their lives. The hand that rocks the cradle really does rule the world!

I believe we all carry some kind of excess baggage we need to let go of. What it is made up of is different for each one of us. Most of us, if we are really honest, carry some notion that we are not enough of something—not good enough, not smart enough, not thin enough, not kind enough, not honest enough, not rich enough, not spiritual enough and we often make these feelings someone else's fault!

I believe if we were supposed to be more of something, or different, we would have been created that way. We need to accept that we are the person we were created to be. It is what it is.

We all receive messages about ourselves very early in our life which have a way of sticking with us. Often, we find a way to blame someone else for our feelings. I can't even begin to relay the stories I have heard from seniors who are still lamenting with great heaviness their childhood painful memories.

We don't seem to teach the little people about how to let go. We relay the "sticks and stones" fairytale, but everyone knows that words can and do harm us and we carry many of them for a lifetime. We need to practice the art of letting go. More importantly, we need to model it!

We give away our power at a young age and, sometimes, we never get it back. We learn to be angry and spend a lifetime punishing ourselves or others, or both, often in the form of depression and anger. This can take many forms, but all these roads usually lead to empty, sad lives.

As these people grow up and have children of their own, they are prone to pass on the negativity to their children what was modelled for them......and so the generations of low self-esteem and miserable people gets passed on and on, until someone decides to make a change. This can be the beginning of change and health for a family system for generations to come.

We need to take back our power as adults. All of us have had unfair things happen to us –abuse, loss, rejection, bullying, inadequate parents, etc. However, as adults, no matter what negative experiences we may have had, we must take responsibility for the fact that, as adults, we have a choice about how we are going to respond--think, feel and behave – whether or not we are going to try to punish every person we meet to make up for the pain we feel, for what we needed and never got. Whatever happened to forgiveness? Forgiveness helps us not carry the pain anymore, regardless of the behavior of the perpetrator. We do it for ourselves, not for them!

We know the power of our strength when we forgive others who have not asked for it and from whom we will never hear any apology. That's when we find out who we really are. That is the stuff of which character is made.

WE HAVE THE POWER TO CHANGE!!! We need to take back our power. We need to change our thoughts, e.g., "I don't hate my father; I hate that he couldn't give me what I needed; I hate that he doesn't 'get it.'" We need to learn to separate out the person from their behavior. They are not the same. Good people do bad things. Bad people sometimes do good things. We need to learn to use our brains to help us think through things rather than quickly judge the appearance and behaviors of others. If we had lived their life, we might, in fact, behave the same way they do. We need to exercise compassion, forgiveness and love ourselves enough to let their negativity be about them, not about us! This can be life changing!!

We need to learn that the things people say about others really says more about them! Learning this one thing can save lives, prevent suicides, change the world! People everywhere want to be accepted for who they are, but are afraid to be who they are for fear of being rejected. We can't have it both ways!

Perhaps the greatest pain is to feel you are nobody to anybody. These are common feelings in abused children. We often give other people way too much power to control our feelings about ourselves.

Why should we even care about people who won't accept us for who we are? The greatest gift is to be authentically who we really are, regardless of the opinions of others. That's as good as it gets! Isn't it beautiful when someone values us for who we are rather than how they can use us, or what we can do for them?

In truth, there are people and relationships we cannot afford to hang onto. We need to let them go in order to manage and preserve our own mental health and physical well-being. They are toxic to us and we need to let them go in order to move on. Some of them may be in our own family. I still remember a remark I made at my beloved brother's funeral: "He was my greatest cheerleader and my worst critic."

People can be many things to one another. Life is complex and complicated.

Conversely, there may be people who need to let go of us because we are toxic to them. There are so many reasons why relationships end. We may never understand why. Actually, I'm not very good at knowing or explaining "why," but rather choose to focus on "what are we going to do about it?" In other words, I'm less concerned with understanding the reason it happened but rather concerned with coming to terms with it and moving on. People often waste years trying to figure out "Why?"

There may also be toxic behaviors we have adopted that we need to let go. Remember, addictions are formed to help us avoid pain but often become more painful than what they were designed to help us avoid. I don't think we hear enough about destination addiction.

Beware of destination addiction, a preoccupation that your happiness is in the next place, next job, next relationship, next child, next therapist, next weight loss. Happiness must be found where you are, who you are. We always have to begin with the truth of who and where we are. That is where change begins. The grass really isn't greener on the other side. We always have to begin from where we really are, not where we wish we were. We need to own our reality.

There are trained, caring people who will help us with these issues if we ask. These are the lucky ones, the ones who want to become healthier and lead more productive lives, be a better companion, a better parent, a better human being. I respect the courage it takes to sign onto the challenge of change. It takes courage to ask for help.

When I had a private practice, with a new patient, I would sometimes listen for months to a patient labor on and on endlessly with the negative discourse of their life. At some point, I intervened by asking them if they had any desire or intention of making any changes in their own life. If their answer was 'no,' I did not make any more appointments with them. "Ain't it awful" is a toxic lifestyle. Confession without change is a game!

They were wasting their money and my time. I moved on, whether they did or not!

The process I'm talking about here is a very difficult one. Most people cannot afford to be in therapy for long periods of time which is why self-help books have become so popular. My concept of therapy is that we peel off a layer at a time, often grieving at the reality of it, and we learn to move on. Letting go is very hard to do.

We own our pain and then work on letting it go, replacing it with healing positive alternatives. Then we move to the next layer, and the next. I have concluded over many years of doing this that therapy, much like life, will always be unfinished business.

I am still working on old issues that resurface from time to time and I have to practice the same process I work at teaching others. It is endless, but so worthwhile. The alternative is settling for a life I do not want to live. If I had made that choice, I would not be writing this book.

Reframing, then, is a very powerful tool we can learn to use to start taking back our power and empower ourselves to live our best life. Do an assessment of your filter and ask yourself if there are things you might need to change.

We can learn to let go and not look back! We don't have to live in our past anymore! We need to lay that burden down, let it go, and move on. It's time to do the post-mortem and let it go! It is what it is!

CHAPTER FOUR
Accepting the Challenges

Reality can be a formidable opponent.

Not being loved by someone we counted on is one of the most painful challenges, as is losing a child or a mate, a loved one or feeling betrayed by a good friend. They all leave their mark on us. Loss is very painful, no matter what form it takes.

Not only must we understand the concept that we can't un-ring the bells, we must understand that the bells continue to ring throughout our lives.

Every new developmental phase of our lives offers new challenges in managing the ringing of the bells. From childhood through old age, the bells will ring. We don't deal with them once and move on. It is a never-ending challenge of facing each of the markers in our lives as they happen.

We can't face what we haven't identified.

Which bells have rung in your life?: the bell of rejection, failure, addictions, loss? What are your most painful memories? What are your greatest fears, based on your experiences? What are your greatest strengths? What do you need that you aren't getting? What does someone need from you that they aren't getting?

What kind of 'aha' moments do you fantasize happening if you were to keep a journal and hike the Appalachian trail? (It takes 5 months and is over 2,000 miles long; less than 10 % of those who start it complete it!). If I were much younger, I would add this to my bucket list. I believe this would be a fabulous experience to have. Some war veterans suffering from post-traumatic-stress-syndrome are taking up the challenge of hiking the trail and some say it has saved their lives!

I loved the movie, "A Walk in the Woods," with Nick Nolte and Robert Redford who decide to tackle the trail late in their lives. I loved hearing all of their insights about themselves and their lives as they experienced the challenge. Most of us stay too busy to make those kinds of observations and insights.

When you have alone time, do you allow whatever is deep within you to come to the surface, or do you shove it back where it came from? This is a defense known as repression or suppression (unconscious or conscious) and sucks a lot of emotional energy from us. Similarly, our dreams are said to be messages from our unconscious and that we can learn a lot about ourselves from paying attention to them. There even exists a form of therapy known as dream therapy.

We have to face our fears. We have to identify them and own them. Then we can work on letting them go. I sometimes ask myself the question, "What's the worst thing that could happen?" This sometimes makes it easier to face. In truth, I doubt there are many people whose lives turned out the way they planned.

What are your fantasies about how you will feel when you come to the end of your life? What will be your regrets--your victories and proudest moments? What will be your legacy? Have you ever written your epitaph? What are you leaving behind? How will the world or some person be different because of your life? What difference do you want to make? What do you still have on your bucket list? Are you making any plans to complete it? What are you waiting for? What message do you imagine on your headstone? What do you see between the dash of your birthdate to your date of death? What stands out for you?

End of life challenges are not often discussed. Yet, these are the very issues that many people want to work on in therapy. In the end, how are you going to feel about yourself? What do you want to do about it while you still have some time and energy left? What are you waiting for? Right now, someone is taking their last breath, wishing they still had time to make changes, but the clock has run out. Don't let that be your story.

I have spent a fair amount of time with people facing death. At times, death has felt like a gift because it brings to the surface the truth of what people really care about. Sometimes, it is a time when people discover who they really are. Sometimes it is a time of extreme regret for what was never even attempted, let alone accomplished.

Those who seem to fear death the least are the ones who feel the best about the lives they have lived. They seem to have a kind of peace about making the transition out of this world. Often, people die the way they have lived. Others are terrified and die screaming for others to help them. It is too late.

Living with the reality of the bells has to include the ring of death. It is inevitable. It will come to each of us. How do we manage the bell of death? One way is by living, being, doing our best, never giving up.

I once lived with a dear friend for the last year of her life and watched her die one day at a time. We talked about death nearly every day. We cried and lamented leaving her 3 children, at the young age of 45. Part of her reality at that time was to simply put one foot in front of the other and trust the ground to be there. I've never forgotten her wise words. When her time came, I gripped her hand in mine, told her it was "O.K to go" and gently closed her eyes. I don't think I could ever do that for anyone again. That bell rang for me vicariously, and very painfully. What an incredible best friend she was. I haven't had one like her since and probably never will again.

None of us lead perfect lives, not even close. It's two steps forward, three steps back, etc. But, each of us has the right to decide what winning the game of life looks like to us. I respect that. It has taken me a very long time to understand this concept--that people have every right to decide for themselves what their path will look like. After all, they are the ones who will have to take responsibility and be accountable for it. It is a serious choice. It is the most important one we will ever make.

As a mental health professional, I am constantly challenged to understand the balance between what I believe to be a healthy path and to understand that people will make different choices than the ones I see. This is especially difficult for those closest to us. Yet, life goes on and we find some kind of way to adjust to allowing children to grow up and find their own way. The only person we really get to decide for is ourselves. That is a big chunk of reality to digest! No matter who we think we manage to control, in the end, we only control ourselves. Children grow up and take control of their own lives, make their own choices, decide who they want to be and the life they choose to live.

The challenges will always be there. Things will not always work out the way we wanted. People won't always give us what we want from them, won't do what we want, won't live their lives the way we think they should. The challenge is not for us to decide for others what is right, but to accept the challenge to accept it for ourselves. I have to forgive myself for something nearly every day of my life! I've had to accept there are goals I will never reach, qualities I will never acquire. I have had to lower a lot of my expectations of myself and others.

At this stage of my life, what I seem to want most for myself is a peaceful setting in nature. That is where I am most comfortable. I think we must follow our heart, must be congruent with our inner wisdom in order to be at peace.

I find that I am only beginning to understand that I, too, have to cope with the bells of 'vicarious trauma' and 'secondary post-traumatic stress' from my many, many years of doing my work. I did not see this coming.

It has only been much later that I have realized how many of my defenses I have used up. I am not as well defended now and could not, at this point in my life, continue the work I once did.

I am an ENFP (extrovert, intuitive, feeling, perceiving) on the Meyers-Briggs Personality Test. I am one of the fun people. I was married over thirty years, raised three sons, travelled the world and got to do more than I ever dreamed possible. All of this became my reality because of all the wonderful people God blessed me with who helped me on my journey, who took the time, who believed in me and empowered me. I hope I'm on someone's list as being one of those people on their journey. What greater honor?

I grew up in a family, the youngest of three children with a mother who never finished high school. She was such a treasure in my life, and one of the wisest women I ever knew and I remember her telling me, "An education is something no one can take away from you." She taught me survival skills I continue to use and treasure.

I am not a stranger to pain. My desire to overcome it started at a very early age. I am grateful I accepted the challenge of deciding for myself what life I would choose. I am so grateful for the gifts I was given: a very loving Mother, the gift of faith in a loving God, a good brain, a love for learning. I am grateful for teachers along the way who believed in me and encouraged me to put on a wide-angle lens and make healthy choices about my life. We never know when we have planted a seed that will make a positive difference in someone else's life. We just have to do/be what we can, and let it be enough.

On the other hand, I have met some who would say it is easier not to accept the challenge of living the best life. It is too much work. It isn't fun. It isn't impressive, but rather that it's fine to have a heart full of hate and use it to desecrate anything you choose, Including children, animals, or anything else that gets in your way. I've seen this lifestyle in action more than I wanted. It is not pretty. It is destructive, like a cancer, as it spreads to so many others who deserve better. These are the ones who use people and love things, and want everyone to suffer!

I have stared into the eyes of evil on more than one occasion. It was about as much reality as I ever want to see. I will never forget it.

This was an intense reality for me. I once asked a mass murderer what it felt like to kill another person. His reply, "My hand got so tired." This man made a choice about his response to the bells that had rung in his life. This was a very loud ring of reality in my career. I realized he would likely have snapped my neck in half in a heart-beat if given the chance. Actually, I have had my life threatened by a mentally ill inmate and it is during those times that you find of what stuff you are made. It is most challenging for the majority of us to understand that not everyone sees the world through our eyes. We cannot usually second-guess people. They are far more complex than most of us understand.

I once stood on death row in a prison. You could hear a pin drop. I felt as though a tidal wave of evil swept over me and I couldn't get out of there fast enough. I was standing outside the cells of several men who had kidnapped and killed children. I couldn't help but think of the challenge I felt to differentiate between evil and mental illness. I hate them both. I am only well-trained to deal with mental illness, not with the challenges of evil.

Most of us live somewhere between death row and the Brady Bunch. Regardless of where we live, we have to make a choice about whether or not we want to take up the gauntlet of deciding to accept the challenge of dealing with the real issues of our lives or settle for a detour that will get us to the end of our lives. I call it the "useless but familiar" path. Unfortunately, I have trafficked for a very long time at the seamy end of society and grieved over choices I watched other people make. Nonetheless, it was my choice to be there.

There are prices to be paid for our choices. We must carefully look at the price tag before making our decisions. Our decisions change us, and often change others as well.

Unfortunately, the experience usually comes first and the lesson comes later.

CHAPTER FIVE
Getting Serious About the Bells

"Life is like a basketball....
You can take a shot or dribble it away."

Getting serious about working on your issues is a courageous decision. It will likely change you. If I could bequeath one gift to the human race, it would be for every person to desire to be and pursue the very best life possible for themselves.

Think of one thing in your life you would like to change. Think about seeking out a professional of some sort to help make that change. Do not be shy about shopping around for the right person to help you. Don't settle for someone who doesn't really work for you.

You need to be comfortable with the person you are going to entrust your innermost thoughts, desires and fears.

I spent about three years in therapy. Part of it was a requirement for obtaining a Ph.D. in Clinical Psychology. Actually, I believe it was an excellent assignment to have to sit on the other side of the desk and really experience the angst of being the patient. This is serious business. Actually, I recall that I used to really look forward to my own therapy sessions where I could focus just on myself and my own issues. It was my time!

However, when I reached out and contacted a therapist on my own because I needed help with a crisis that didn't concern my becoming a psychologist, it was much more personal and much harder. In fact, it was some of the hardest work I ever did in my life. It was so grueling that I once walked out of a session because the pain became so great. I can't even begin to describe how completely shredded I felt before I finally felt put back together again.

I had a mirror held up to me that I neither liked nor appreciated and I made certain that my Johns-Hopkins trained psychiatrist earned every blessed cent he charged. I know I was a very difficult patient. He once told me at the beginning, "If you weren't hurting so badly, I'd tell you to go to hell." I never forgot that. It actually represented the beginning of my exploring the bell of anger, where I learned it, why I stored it, and what I was going to have to do to let go of it. It cost me things which were extremely painful for me. I grew up believing that marriage was sacred and those vows were not to be broken. It felt like the saddest day of my life.

As I've indicated, therapy and the decision to make changes in your life may cost you things you never thought possible, so consider long and hard before you take this step seriously. It can be very stressful to move outside of your comfort zone.

I believe there is something in all of us that directs us toward pursuing a path where we can be the best we can be. Every person must know this in his heart. In fact, as one cardiologist put it, we must all follow our heart. It took me many years to understand what he meant.

In fact, I have discovered in these last years of processing my life that I have come to understand so much that I previously just intellectualized. There is such a difference, and I'm so eternally grateful that I lived long enough to 'get it,' at least some of it.

It's funny, once you 'get it,' it isn't nearly so important anymore what anyone else thinks about you. It simply doesn't matter. What matters is that you 'get it.' That's what really matters. It is all about YOUR truth, no one else's.

Having to neither explain yourself nor worry what others think about you is a rare kind of freedom that most of us seek but few reach. In fact, I've heard it said that it's really none of our business what others think of us.

CHAPTER SIX
Being Up Close and Personal

"I thought I grew,
but here I am again..."

I believe most of the world is unfamiliar with the inner workings of mental health professionals. Having been in that career has been a very challenging and rewarding part of my life. It also has been an intriguing experience for me as I reflect on many of my experiences as a mental health professional. They have changed me.

Some are not able to sustain the strength required for this profession and succumb to tragic outcomes. I will never forget an Easter Sunday where I was given the task of calling every patient of a prominent Clinical Psychologist who had chosen to end his life. I will not forget the screaming and shrieking I endured on the phone, all the while feeling fully empathic at their pain, but very angry at the person who created the pain. They had lost the person they depended upon. Clearly, knowing isn't doing.

I spent nearly a year working with his wife to recover from this incident. Fortunately, she was open to working on her anger and pain and I was proud of the work she did to deal with the ringing of that bell and the intense consequences for her and her baby daughter. What a tragedy.

Suicide in America is a much larger problem than people want to admit. It is a leading cause of death among young people in America. When I was studying for my National Psychology Board Exams, the highest group registering suicides was ages 9-11. I could hardly believe it.

Just this week, I have learned of another young person's suicide which has devastated her family. I am aware of a study which declares, almost without reservation, that there are very discernable signs of the intentions of people who plan to take their lives. If people are paying attention and listening carefully, the signs are there.

Unfortunately, it is the people who talk about it who follow through. Also, after one attempt, the risk goes even higher. We all need to be paying more attention to despondent people, people who are unable, for whatever reason, to come to terms with the ringing of the bell. We need to try to help them if we can. Actually, just being there and listening is a very powerful form of help. We all need to understand that people do give up. People have a breaking point. Death can be seductive!

Losing a child, being diagnosed with a personal illness, being served with divorce papers, finding out you've been deceived throughout your life, spending the rest of your life on death row--the list of bells rung goes on and on. Everyone has a breaking point. Sometimes death looks easier. In truth, there are probably days when everyone feels death would be easier!

I've always wondered if we could interview all of the inmates on death row (and there are many hundreds of them in this country) what mental health professionals could learn that could make a difference in the way we help people. Such a study needs to happen. How, what are the reasons that all those people ended up at the same place? Why? What are the common variables? What could we come to understand that we could teach in families and schools that could make a difference? I doubt that study will ever happen. I hope I'm wrong.

At the end of the day, as I reflect on all the bells that have rung in my life, I wish I had managed them better. I ran across a quote which expresses what I feel about my life:

Thanks to those who loved me, you helped me grow. Thanks to those who hated me, you made me strong. Thanks to those who cared, you made me feel I mattered. Thanks to those who entered my life and made me who I am today. Thanks to those who left me, teaching me that nothing lasts forever. Thanks to those who stayed and showed me true friendship. Thanks to those who listened, you made me feel I was worth it. (Anonymous)

I've worked in a lot of places. I've been a guest speaker at the FBI Headquarters in Quantico, Virginia. I've written two previous books. I have acquired four college degrees, raised 3 sons and was married more than 30 years. God has richly blessed my life, in spite of all the painful bells. Even so, if I'm really honest, I have to admit that I wouldn't wish my life on anyone.

Now, nearing the end of my journey, I find myself thinking long and hard about my choices, where I want to live and how I want to spend the time I have left. I want to contemplate and meditate on the many ways God has blessed my life. I am drawn to peace, the Prince of Peace.

I continuously reflect on where I've been and where I'm going, where I've been and where I still want to be. I reflect on people I wish I had never met, conversations I wish I had never had, things I wish I had never disclosed, opportunities I wish I hadn't passed up, choices I wish I hadn't made--bells I wish hadn't rung. Mostly, though, I reflect on the good things, the positive things. I get into my 'happy place' which helps me to create a positive place in my mind where I place all the people I love so dearly. I imagine them in a circle in a glass house with a permeating golden loving light that enables me to face most anything. Just thinking about it makes me smile. Perhaps you might want to work on creating a happy place for yourself, one where you experience gratitude, instead of anger and depression, one where you can remember and re-live the best memories of your life, where you can be all you want to be, if only for a moment. Those previews of what we allow ourselves to dream as possible is a very precious place to be. I treasure them.

Speaking of treasures, that's how I feel about animals. I feel so incredibly grateful that God put dogs on the Earth. They have been some of my closest friends. So, in my lovely constructed house of peace, I will, of course, have a special place for my "Max," Westie Extraordinaire.

In my home, I have colors -- reds, purple, green, blue, yellow, turquoise--all the colors of the rainbow. I have beautiful pictures of people and places I've treasured, and I look out at the ocean. The environment we create is very important in impacting our mental health.

What a joy to have taken all of the bells of my life and reduced them to this lifestyle, in spite of the tears, regrets, mistakes, trauma, bruises and scars. I feel so blessed. I actually live in such a place.

Having chosen a "dark" career, I have mixed thoughts as I reflect on that choice. I feel so grateful that I could be a part of helping others in some small way but it took a very long time before I realized the price I paid personally to be in that field. There are a lot easier ways to make a living. I believe it is something we are drawn to for, perhaps, unknown reasons, maybe just because it was meant to be. At any rate, it, too, is what it is. I am still gathering the pieces of the puzzle and making sense of it, probably an unending task...

CHAPTER SEVEN
Thinking: Yes I Can

"...They shall run and not be weary;
they shall walk and not faint."

This book is filled with experiences about my specific journey. Everyone has a story to tell.

While my profession is on the 'dark' side, my whole purpose in communicating my experiences is to offer hope. This is simply my story, another human being trying to find her way, as we all are.

I have tried to be very honest about my feelings and my life rather than share the 'party line' of correct Christian responses. I grew up in what I call the "First Church of the Neurotic" which I have spent a lifetime trying to sort out. It has been very challenging for me to identify and manage the legalism. Another way of expressing this idea is to say that I am often probably not very politically correct! I tend to be very straight-forward, without pretense, what my son calls "bold."

In spite of all of the painful examples, the message here is a very positive one: I am a huge believer in the power of people to be all God created them to be. Many of us simply need help knowing where to look. The intent of my book is to be helpful in encouraging people to believe in themselves, to forgive themselves (and others) and to realize that change is within their power: "Yes I can." I've shared my stories in hopes of encouraging others to believe that change can happen, hearts can heal and life can be enjoyed, not simply endured. God said He came so that we might have life abundantly!

I want people to feel empowered, not powerless, addicted, angry or depressed. My intent is to demonstrate that no matter who you are, what you've done, or what you are dealing with, you can make your life better than it is.

God has created you and has His hand on your life. You can start to believe in yourself again. You can begin to learn that you are not doomed by your past. You can still make choices about your life that will help you feel better about it, better about yourself, more peaceful about your life. You can decide to accept grace for your life. I speak the truth!

When I was working on my M.A. degree in college, I took a self-esteem test. I scored it myself because I knew the results would be poor. I scored in the lower 7 percentile. That meant that 93% of people who had taken this same test had greater self-esteem than I had. This result did not surprise me, although I realized I had learned to cover it. I began asking people who "knew" me where they thought I scored on the test. Most people guessed me to be somewhere in the 90% percentile. It was then that I knew I had to face the fact that I had created a persona that was much different than how I really felt about myself. This was a huge red flag in my life that I wanted to avoid. I didn't share this fact with anyone but, over time, I started making very small changes, baby steps, that led me in a positive direction until I reached some congruence between how I really felt about myself and who I projected myself to be. This took me decades to achieve, but I did it.

I knew the reason I had such low self-esteem.

No one knew that I had a traumatic experience when I was 15 years old. I had an overwhelming encounter of what psychologist John Bradshaw calls "soul murder." The impact was devastating. In the church I attended, there was a visiting evangelist whom I had never met before, invited to speak at a church camp. He, through a series of circumstances, directed some venomous judgment at me and nearly destroyed me. **I didn't even know this man, but I was a very insecure young girl and I internalized it, and carried it for far too long. After all, he claimed to be a representative of God. Had I been physically assaulted, I don't believe this experience could have created any greater trauma for me.**

It wasn't until 16 years later, after I finally had some self-esteem that I saw his picture on a brochure, decided to fly to his city and State, made arrangements to see him and

confronted him. He was in charge of a nation-wide evangelical conference.

When he came to the door and opened it, he looked at least two feet shorter than I remembered him.

He didn't even remember me!!!! So, all of the agonizing years that I had obsessed about this traumatic event was only creating a problem for me, not for him. What a lesson this was.

Slowly, as he began to remember, I watched tears run down his face and heard his apology. I struggled with my feelings as I made my first inroad to forgive him. He passed away many years later. I never saw or had anymore contact with him again.

Sometimes we just have to be patient while God puts our broken hearts back together again, piece by piece.

I was so aware of the enormous damage in the name of God that has happened to many people I have treated in my practice. Somehow, it seems to me to be one of the most cunning forms of evil!

It is so easy to acquire a little bit of power and believe God has designated us to judge the hearts and lives of all the people in the world. As one of my patients put it, "Beware the Christians!" I believe, as a Christian, that the Holy Spirit doesn't need me to do His job for Him. Judgment belongs to Him!

These are very hard lessons to grasp. I know you can't get an advanced degree in the helping profession without understanding how easy it is to hurt people as well as help them. Perhaps Schools of Theology need to teach this truth as well.

I can't help but think of the words of Cory Booker:

Before you speak to me about religion, first show me how you treat other people. Before you tell me how much you love God, first show me how you love His children. Before you preach to me of your passion for your faith, teach me about it through your compassion for others. In the end, I'm not as interested in what you have to tell me about your religion as I am in how you choose to live it.

I have shared this painful example to communicate that our greatest traumas can be managed and overcome. The scar stays with us but it is possible to move on. We must do what we have to, let it go, and learn the lesson.

Had I made a different decision about this traumatic incident, I believe it would have changed my life dramatically. I would never have entered my current profession or ever tried to help anyone. I'm so grateful God directed this process rather than letting it ruin my life as unfinished business. This was a make-or- break event in my life. Perhaps there is one in yours also.

As children, we don't yet have the cognitive capacity nor the defenses to understand that the things people say about others says more about them than the person they are describing.

Even as children, we get caught up in a world that demands we conform, including some churches and homes. We are told how to think, feel and behave and are rarely reinforced for showing any independent thinking of our own. This is one of the reasons I believe teachers are so important. They certainly have had a huge impact on my life. They taught me to begin to believe in myself by reinforcing the essence of who I was as a person. I began to realize that it was O.K. to think my own thoughts, to have an opinion that was different than others and that it was O.K. to express it. It was O.K. to think outside the box. I had to learn also, however, that not everyone was going to like me or what I had to say, or agree with me. But, what kind of life is it to simply go through the motions so that no one dislikes us? That seems to be what so many people have settled for. We give away our power to be all we were created to be and end up often suffering lives of alienation, low self-esteem, addiction and depression. Clearly, this is not our best life. This is not the fulfilling life God has promised us if we put our faith in Him and let Him direct our path.

People need to stop settling for a life and relationships that really are not working. We need to get real about how it really is for us and start working on making some small changes to lead us in the healthy direction we really need to go. Time is marching on. Don't give up on your dreams! Don't give up on yourself. In fact, it's all about getting better, not giving up!

One of the most powerful messages any child can receive is that they are capable of becoming whatever their heart desires if they are willing to do what it takes to get there. They will discover on their own all the challenges, twists and turns of the path it will put them on and they will make the adjustments over time.

There must be a "Yes, I can" message instilled in them from an early age. Otherwise, children won't have the confidence they need to try, and fail at some things, but figure out how to survive the failures. They will also learn that they are not failures, what they tried didn't work. That's all it means--not that they are failures!!! Learning this big difference at an early age is such a powerful tool to have. In fact, I have not observed it in many adults. We must all learn to separate out the person from their behavior, including and especially, ourselves.

Isn't it better to have tried something and failed rather than never to have tried at all? We choose safety over accomplishment. What does that teach us? The bell of failure is an important and powerful bell we all need to make friends with. This is how self-esteem is built and encouraged. We must become free to fail, pick ourselves up, and move on.

My GPA in graduate school was a 3.9 on a 4.0 scale. When I apologized to my graduate advisor he replied by saying, "It will give your record character." I had gotten one B in 4 years of graduate school. Because I had such low self-esteem, I was driven to always try to be the best and get the best grade. He was a wise man. He helped me reframe and gain perspective.

The "Yes I can" attitude is a necessary component for a happy, successful life. You have to believe in yourself! And, if you are lucky enough to have loved ones in your life who reinforce this value, you are especially blessed. However, if you are not lucky enough to have it, then you need to work on gaining it in other ways, but don't give up.

For those without parents or teachers or loved ones who do not provide the love, safety and encouragement when we are children, the climb of the hill is much steeper and much harder, but not impossible. We need to hang onto our power and not let others take away our sense of hope and well-being. My Dad used to tell me that success is best defined by obstacles overcome rather than heights attained!

For me, one of the greatest gifts of my life has been my unshaken belief in a loving God Who has always had His hand on my life, no matter what, even though I didn't always feel it! The power of belief and prayer are the most powerful tools in my toolbox, with my Ph.D's as a close second. God offers so many promises in His Word that He has designed our path, is there to hold our feet to it, and will see us to the end.

> "Trust in the Lord with all your heart and lean not unto your own understanding; In all yours ways, acknowledge Him and He will direct your path." (Proverbs 3:5-6)

Does it get any better than that? And so, it can be within that framework that we can have a quiet assurance deep within our souls, the message of "Yes, I can!" no matter what! That is the assurance of peace God promises.

CHAPTER EIGHT
Making Choices & Reviewing Tools

"Two roads diverged in a wood and I
took the one less travelled by, and that
has made all the difference."
(Robert Frost)

You and I are in charge of making the difference in the two roads that are in front of us. Whichever choice we decide to make, we will never know what our life might have been had we taken the other path. We have to live with that.

We also have to live with the reality that if we don't like our lives, it is up to us to change it. That burden will always rest with us. God gave us free-will.

The challenge of the ringing of the bells and our responding choices is the key to how we shape our lives. We really must own every one of them and own who we really are. That is where we all need to start. It is what it is, whether we like it or not.

Let's review the specific tools that have been laid out in this book, and think about how we can apply them to make life better.

1. You must take time to identify the specific bells that have rung in your life. Don't stay so busy that you are not focused. Then make some notes about how you have managed them. Identify the ones that still need work and make a specific plan to make specific and needed changes. Start today.

2. Consider how or whether or not you have taken responsibility for your part in these events. Be very honest with yourself. If you haven't, start there! No matter how deserving you are to be angry, it is poison to your life and you can't afford to keep it. Do what you have to do to make it right.

3. Use the tool of Reframing in order to better understand the event. Take the views of what other people may have felt (e.g., the adopted child or the hated father I talked about). Think about how you would feel if you walked in their shoes and saw the world as they do. Don't be afraid to admit when you're wrong. That's the beginning of wisdom.

4. Try to separate out the person from their behavior, e.g., making a wrong decision does not make you a bad person. Help your children understand this concept at an early age. Remember to apply it to yourself. We all do things we regret. Use it as a learning tool to make changes. Practice forgiving yourself, and others. Doing a bad thing is not the same as being a bad person. Teach this to your children.

5. Remember things that are said say more about the person making the statement than anyone else. Make it a point to observe who says what to whom with what effect? Stay away from making judgmental negative remarks. That is not your job.

6. Strongly consider your options as you seek to manage and reconcile the bells in your life. Is an apology needed? Is forgiveness needed? Is there something you still need to do in order to let it go and move on? Do you need to make amends with anyone? Start today.

7. Ask yourself what you are pretending not to know. Take a hard look at toxic people, thoughts, feelings and behaviors in your life. Make a plan to begin changing what you need. Begin by changing your thoughts. The feelings and behavior will follow. This is crucial to making lasting changes.

8. Examine any detours you are using in your life to help you avoid certain bells because of people, traits, faults in your life you don't want to deal with. Which detours, e.g., food, drugs, nicotine, alcohol, etc. are you choosing? What price is it costing you to be on that detour? How is it affecting your relationships with your family, friends and co-workers? Deal with it!

9. Assess whether or not you need to make changes and if you do, ask for help. Believe in

yourself that you are capable of making any change you choose. Commit to it and make it happen. Let others help and support you.

10. Always have the mindset of "Yes I can." If you don't believe in yourself, how will anyone else?

11. Giving up is never an option! If you feel like giving up, tell someone. Ask for help.

12. Stop blaming others and yourself for your pain. That is not productive. It really doesn't matter whose fault it is. You can reframe, change and move on from whatever is the source of your pain. Believe it!

13. Consider what positive bells you have the power to still ring for yourself and for others? Get creative! Make fun plans. Find the joy in your life. Be the joy in someone's else's. Be a seed-planter!

14. Enjoy your life. Do something nice for yourself every day. Practice random acts of kindness. Create the kind of life for yourself you wish someone would create for you. Be the friend you need. You can do this.

15. You are not alone. You have a Divine Creator who loves you unconditionally, understands you better than anyone else and is on call 24/7 for you. Believe it!

16. Take a look at how you perceive your personal power. Are you giving it away in ways that defeat you. What would it look like for you to take it back?

17. Don't be afraid of the bell of death. Remember, people tend to die the way they have lived. When that time comes, go out with as few regrets as possible. Manage the bells in your life as best you can, rest, and be at peace.

If we would all work on each of these 17 steps, it could be life-changing, produce happier and more productive lives, give us a different world. The key rests with our choices!

It seems we have been given a great deal of power. It is all up to us to choose how to use it. And, since none of us know how many years we are going to have, we don't know for sure how long we are going to have to make choices. We are all running out of time.

Life is NOW. It is true that life is what happens to us while we are making other plans. (By the way, have you noticed there are no u-hauls on the back of hearses?)

This leaves us with the ball squarely in our courts.

We can choose to spend a lifetime in denial, anger and depression, blaming someone else for our unhappiness, living on a detour, or a lifetime working on them and formulating a life the best we know how. The choice is ours. We can play the part of the victim, but the power to choose is our call. Remember, we ARE our choices!

There is nothing greater than the power to choose. We have it. We live it. We use it every single day of our lives, until our last. We have all been given the gift, and the responsibility, of making choices. However, make no mistake, one day, our power to make choices will be over.

We can choose peace. We can choose doing the right things for the right reasons. We can choose love. We can choose giving. We can choose making a positive difference in someone's else's life, and in our own. We can choose forgiveness. We can choose to be our own best friend, to nurture ourselves in order to nurture others, including beloved pets. We can make a contribution to making the world a better place, by being a better person.

Then, it can be within a framework of gratitude and peace that we have the confidence that we have run the race of life as best we knew and we can slide into home plate with a bang, not a whimper.

I've heard it said that a good life is when we assume nothing, do more, need less, smile often, dream big, laugh more and realize how blessed we are.

Perhaps that lifestyle will lead us toward confronting all the bells in our lives, with gratitude, hope and a sense of well-being, that will bring us peace as we leave the Earth, and empower us to be all we can be, and to help others do the same.

So, when it's our turn, I believe we can take our last breath, as we transition, thinking "Yes I can," as we hear that last bell:

"Never send to know for whom the bell tolls,
it tolls for thee."
(John Donne)

The last bell has rung and we now exist only in someone's memory. Our time for choices has come and gone.

May our memory bring a smile and a smoother pathway for someone behind us who knew us and was made the better for it.

*****

Printed in the United States
By Bookmasters